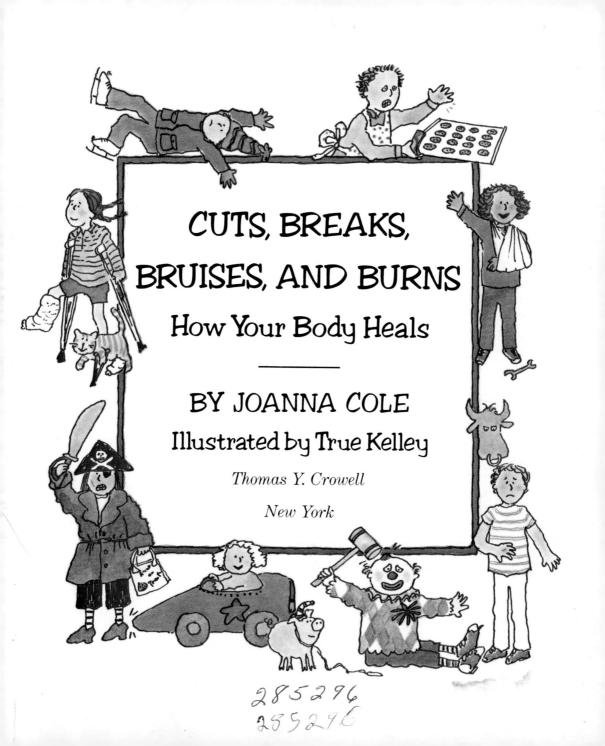

CUTS, BREAKS, BRUISES, AND BURNS

How Your Body Heals

BY JOANNA COLE

Illustrated by True Kelley

Thomas Y. Crowell

New York

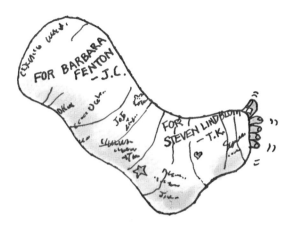

Acknowledgments

The author thanks Dr. Russell Ross, Professor of Pathology at the University of Washington School of Medicine and a researcher in the field of wound healing, for reviewing the manuscript and illustrations.

Thanks also to Rodney Hite, M.D., a practicing pediatrician in New York City, for reading the manuscript, and to William F. Goetz, M.D., of Bellevue Emergency Services, for his helpful consultation.

For reviewing the first-aid section, the author is grateful to Mary Marotta, R.N.

Cuts, Breaks, Bruises, and Burns: How Your Body Heals
Text copyright © 1985 by Joanna Cole
Illustrations copyright © 1985 by True Kelley
All rights reserved. No part of this book may be used or reproduced in any manner whatsoever without written permission except in the case of brief quotations embodied in critical articles and reviews. Printed in the United States of America. For information address Thomas Y. Crowell Junior Books, 10 East 53rd Street, New York, N.Y. 10022. Published simultaneously in Canada by Fitzhenry & Whiteside Limited, Toronto.
1 2 3 4 5 6 7 8 9 10
First Edition

Library of Congress Cataloging in Publication Data
Cole, Joanna.
  Cuts, breaks, bruises, and burns.

  Summary: Explains how specialized cells in the body function to heal simple wounds and injuries.
  1. Wound healing—Juvenile literature. 2. Blood cells—Juvenile literature. [1. Wound healing.
2. Blood cells] I. Kelley, True, ill. II. Title.
RD94.C65 1985   612   84-45335
ISBN 0-690-04437-2
ISBN 0-690-04438-0 (lib. bdg.)

Contents

Your Body Heals Itself

You will probably get many cuts, scrapes, bruises and burns in your lifetime. You might even break a bone or two. No matter how many minor injuries you get, they always heal. Your cut closes, your bruise fades away, your bone mends. But it doesn't happen by magic. It is your body itself that works to repair the damage.

Not Just a Machine

In some ways your body is like a machine. Your joints move like hinges, your heart works like a pump, even your brain is something like a computer. But there are some important differences. One of these is that when your body is injured, it does not need to be repaired like a machine. It can repair itself, because it is alive.

Your body is made of billions of tiny living cells. These cells are so small they can be seen only under a microscope. There are many kinds of cells in the body. They have different shapes and sizes, and they do different jobs, but they all are made of a jelly-like material called protoplasm, surrounded by a cell membrane. There are cells in every part of your body.

Even your blood has cells. Red blood cells carry oxygen to all parts of your body and give the blood its red color. There are other kinds of cells in the blood too. Some of these act like an army on standby, ready to protect you from disease or injury.

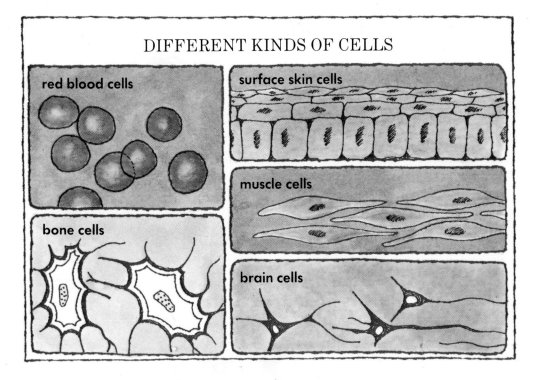

DIFFERENT KINDS OF CELLS

red blood cells

surface skin cells

muscle cells

bone cells

brain cells

Please Do NOT PET THE BULL

How a Cut Heals

You are climbing a fence when a sharp edge cuts your finger. You yell, "OW!" and pull back your hand. The sharp edge has cut through two levels of skin: the surface layer of your skin, called the epidermis, and the inner layer, the dermis. The dermis contains nerves—which are sensitive to pain, heat and touch—and microscopic blood vessels called capillaries.

Even though you know the cut will heal, you still might feel a little scared when you see blood coming out. But the blood itself contains the substances needed to heal the cut. Like a microscopic rescue team, special cells are already at work.

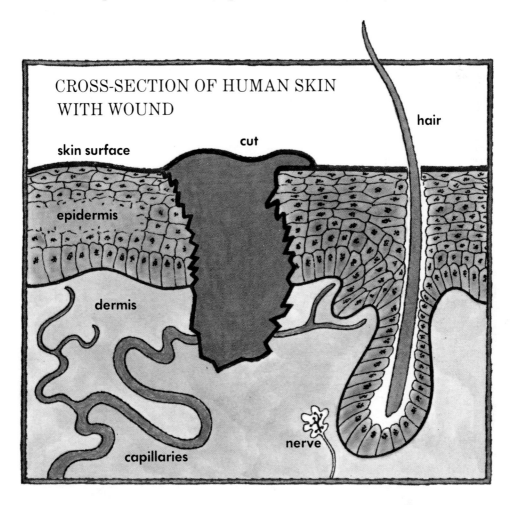

CROSS-SECTION OF HUMAN SKIN WITH WOUND

hair

cut

skin surface

epidermis

dermis

capillaries

nerve

Stopping the Bleeding

First to the rescue are tiny blood cells called platelets. Usually, platelets flow smoothly through the bloodstream. But when they touch a rough surface—such as the edges of a broken or cut blood vessel—the platelets change. They become sticky. They stick to the edges of the injured vessels. More and more platelets flow to the vessels. They pile up until they form a clump that acts like a plug. That is why a small cut stops bleeding all by itself in a minute or two. If the body did not have its own way of plugging leaks, you could lose all your blood from even a small cut.

THREE STAGES
OF STOPPING
THE BLEEDING

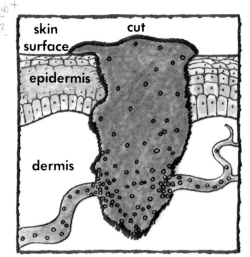

1. Platelet plug forms

After the bleeding has stopped, your cut is still filled with liquid blood. Now this blood starts to clot, or coagulate; that is, it changes from a liquid to a jelly-like substance called a clot. In the clot, tiny fibers (thread-like strands) form a net that holds the sides of the cut together. This net helps keep the cut from opening and starting to bleed again.

After several hours, the surface of the clot dries out. It becomes a scab. You may not think of a scab as useful, but it is actually an important part of the healing process. The scab acts like a hard shield that protects the injured area.

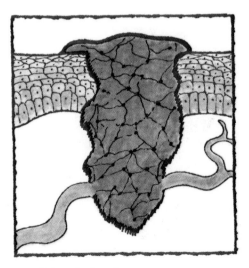

2. *Blood clot forms*

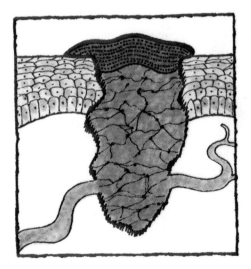

3. *Scab forms*

Underneath the scab, the healing really begins. Other blood cells start entering the cut from nearby blood vessels. These new cells are the white blood cells. They are able to destroy bacteria, or germs, and to carry away bits of dirt.

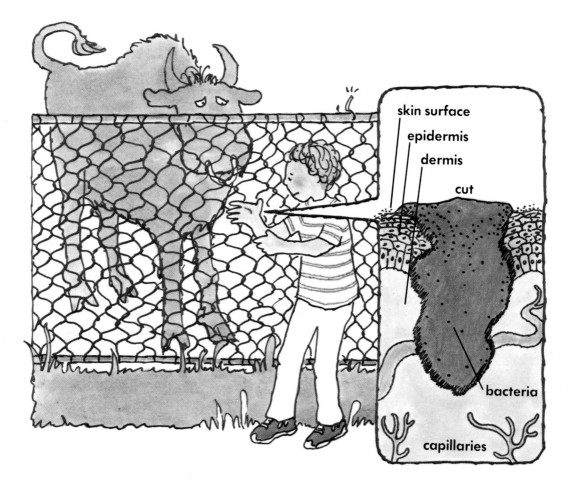

Fighting the Invaders

Almost every cut has bacteria and dirt in it. The sharp edge of a fence, for example, may have been brushed by an animal, which left bacteria on it. Bits of dust and soil, too small for us to see, are on it too. When you cut yourself on the fence, some of the bacteria and dirt get into the cut.

The white blood cells, which destroy dirt and bacteria, are different from other cells in your body. For one thing, they can "swim." To do this, part of the cell pushes out like an arm in one direction. Then the rest of the cell flows into it. Another "arm" reaches out, and the cell body follows. In this way, a white blood cell can swim through the blood.

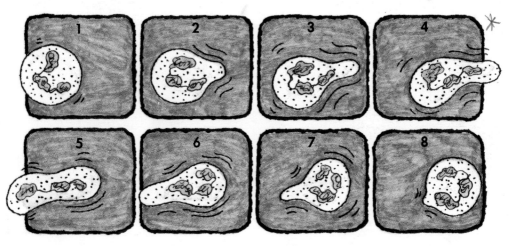

HOW A WHITE BLOOD CELL "SWIMS"

When you hurt yourself, white blood cells travel to the blood vessels near the cut. In order to do its job, a white cell needs to get out of the vessel and swim into the damaged area. It does this by pushing an "arm" between the cells that make up the blood vessel wall. In a few minutes, the whole white cell squeezes through.

Once they are free, the white cells swim into the cut. There they actually begin eating bacteria and particles of dirt by engulfing them—drawing them inside their cell membranes.

When the bacteria are inside, they are broken down by digestive juices that are very similar to those used to digest food in your stomach.

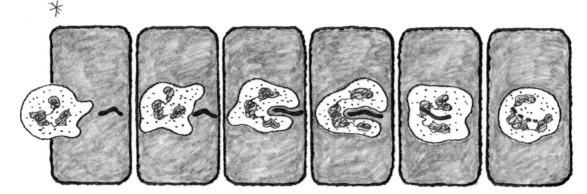

HOW A WHITE BLOOD CELL EATS A BACTERIUM

14

All this is happening without your even being aware of it. You may be going to school, eating lunch, or reading a book, and all the time an invisible battle is going on inside you!

But still the cut is not fully healed. A cut not only opens up the body to bacteria that must be destroyed. It also causes damage that must be repaired. As the white cells continue their work, other cells begin to repair the gap left in the body's surface.

Repairing the Damage

Up to now, the gap has been covered by the scab. Now surface skin cells at the edges of the cut actually begin sliding under the scab to form a layer of new skin over the cut. To get to the open area, skin cells will even slide over each other. Then other skin cells replace them by multiplying—splitting in half to form new cells.

Meanwhile, the white cells have been finishing up their work of killing the bacteria. Now a new kind of white cell enters the wound. These are the "undertakers," or clean-up crew. They eat up old fibers, bits of damaged cells and dead

THREE STAGES
OF REPAIRING
THE DAMAGE

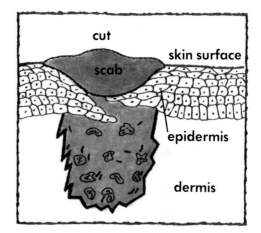

1. Skin cells grow under scab

white cells from the first crew, the bacteria-eating cells, which live only a few days.

By this time the cut is clean, and a very thin layer of surface skin has formed. But the damaged area under it in the inner layer of the skin—the dermis—is still not repaired. Now long thin cells—fibroblasts or "fiber-makers"—start arriving from the surrounding skin. These cells manufacture strands of tough flexible material called collagen, which form a kind of bridge to bind the edges of the gap together.

In about a week the cut is almost completely repaired, and the scab sloughs off. For a while the fiber-makers keep working to strengthen the area with bundles of collagen.

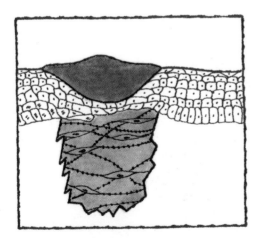

2. *Fibroblasts make fibers*

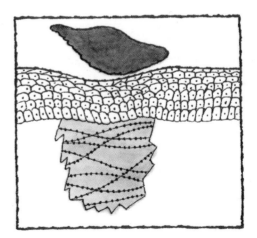

3. *Scab sloughs off*

A newly healed cut often looks pink for a time, especially in a light-skinned person. This is because many new blood vessels were formed during the healing process to bring healing blood to the area. The surface skin is thinner than usual right after healing, so the extra amount of blood is quite visible through the new skin.

As time passes, the extra blood vessels gradually disappear. More and more skin cells are added to the surface layer, and eventually the skin becomes as thick as it was before. Then you are no longer able to see the place where the cut was.

When you know how an ordinary small cut heals, you know how almost every injury heals: First the bleeding is stopped. Then various kinds of cells work to clean up dirt and kill bacteria. Finally the damaged area is rebuilt. Serious injuries take longer to heal than minor ones, but the healing process is the same for a tiny paper cut, a skinned knee or a deadly bullet wound.

Why a Cut Gets Red and Sore

Soon after it stops bleeding, a cut often becomes inflamed. If you see "flame" in that word, there is good reason. Inflamed skin is red and hot, and it is often swollen and sore too. Inflammation is not pleasant, but it actually helps the body heal the injury.

Inflamed skin looks red because of the extra blood that is flowing to it, bringing the healing cells. Because blood is warmer than skin, the skin's temperature goes up, and it feels hot. Since more blood will go to a larger cut, a more serious injury will seem hotter. You probably won't be able to feel the extra heat in a small one, but it will be there just the same.

In addition to getting red and hot, an injury often swells up too. Swelling is caused when plasma, the clear fluid part of blood, leaks out of nearby blood vessels. The plasma brings healing chemicals to the area, and provides a "pool" for the white blood cells to swim in after they leave the blood vessels.

An inflamed cut feels sore as well. This is because cells damaged by the injury release chemicals that stimulate nerve cells and cause pain. Even though pain is unpleasant, it is your body's way of telling you to be careful. The pain reminds you to keep an injured part still so that it can rest and heal.

Because more cells are damaged in a larger injury, it will usually hurt more than a small one, sending you a more urgent message to rest the injured part. Surprisingly, though, some tiny cuts can hurt a lot. Have you ever had a paper cut? Doctors say it is not the cut itself that causes the pain, but the chemicals in the paper. They stimulate nerves and cause stinging. The same thing will happen if you get a small cut and then eat an orange. If juice gets in the cut, the acid in the juice will make the cut sting.

How a Cut Gets Infected

Most cuts heal in about a week—sometimes sooner. But some cuts become infected. That is, they are red and sore for a longer time, and they may get worse before they get better. This is because there are more bacteria and dirt in the cut than the white blood cells can get rid of. The body keeps sending more and more white cells to kill off the bacteria, and the cut stays red and inflamed until they do the whole job.

If a cut is very badly infected, the bacteria could spread to the rest of your body, and you could get sick.

That is why it is important to wash dirty cuts and scrapes with running water. And that is why it is not a good idea to pick off a scab—that leaves the raw wound open to invasion by more dirt and bacteria.

A tight, soggy bandage makes a breeding ground for bacteria. That is why it is best to leave small cuts open to the air. If you need a Band-Aid or bandage to protect a larger wound, change it often.

When a small cut heals smoothly, the clean-up crew eats up the leftover white cells and other debris, and then everything is carried away in the bloodstream to be disposed of as body wastes.

With a badly infected cut, however, things are different. Once it has started to mend, there may be millions of dead white cells left over. Instead of leaving by way of the blood, they stick together and form a white, gooey material, which we call pus. As the healing takes place the pus is pushed up and out of the wound. Such an eruption of pus—once soreness, redness and swelling have started to go away—usually means the infection has been conquered and repairs are under way.

NoTe It is important to take extra care when cuts get infected. If you have a cut that does not look better in two or three days, call your doctor for advice.

What Causes a Scar?

When a wound is so deep or wide that its edges cannot touch as it heals, a visible scar may form. Scar tissue is made of collagen, the tough material manufactured by the fibroblasts (the fiber-maker cells that rebuild all injuries). In smaller cuts we cannot see the small amount of collagen fiber that forms beneath the surface skin. In a larger wound, however, so much fiber is needed to fill the gap that it is visible, and we call it a scar.

Because scar tissue is made of fibers, not skin cells, it is stronger than ordinary skin. Unlike skin, it does not have hairs, sweat glands or blood vessels. It may look shiny and is often a different color from the skin around it.

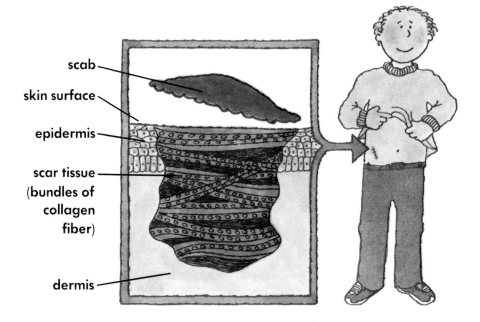

scab

skin surface

epidermis

scar tissue
(bundles of
collagen
fiber)

dermis

Why Are Stitches Used?

A glass breaks on the kitchen floor, and you cut your foot. You press the cut with a clean cloth, but ten minutes later it is still bleeding. Your parents call the doctor, who tells them you may need stitches.

Stitches, or sutures, are used to keep the edges of a wound together. Holding the edges together helps prevent scars, lessens bleeding and reduces the chances of infection.

A doctor usually sews a wound together with a needle and silk or nylon thread. Once the edges have fused, or healed together, the doctor removes the stitches.

Instead of stitches, some doctors and hospitals are using a new kind of staple. These are put in with a plier-like machine.

A doctor may close a smaller wound with strips of thin tape. These are called butterflies, because they are shaped like butterfly wings.

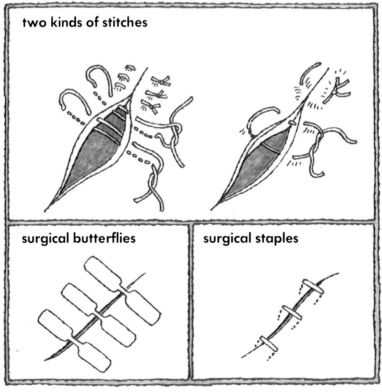

two kinds of stitches

surgical butterflies

surgical staples

HOLDING A WOUND TOGETHER

What Is a Bruise?

A bruise is nothing more than a closed wound—an injury that doesn't break the skin. When you bump yourself, or when you are hit with a heavy object, tiny blood vessels in the inner skin may be broken. The blood drips to a lower level of the skin and forms a pool. This pool of blood is the bruise.

Since the bruise is made of blood, why does it look blue or purple instead of red? It is because the skin acts a little like sunglasses, which change the color of things when you look through them. Through a thin layer of skin, blood looks pink. Through a thicker layer, it looks blue, purple or blackish. A person's cheeks look pink because we can see the blood in the capillaries—the tiny vessels in the inner layer of the skin. But a vein in your arm is deeper, and so it looks blue, even though it is full of red blood. The deeper a bruise is, the darker it looks.

Your natural skin color will also affect the color of a bruise. If your skin is light, a bruise will look blue or purple. If you have darker skin, it will look dark purple, dark blue or black.

A bruise heals when the spilled red blood cells are cleaned up by white cells. It takes the white cells a while to eat up all the red cells, and that is why a bruise goes away slowly.

Have you ever noticed that bruises turn yellow and even green before they heal? This is especially easy to see when a bruise is very large. There are so many spilled red cells that it takes the clean-up crew a long time to clear them away. The red cells begin to decay, and as they do, they change colors. Eventually, however, they are all cleaned up, and the skin returns to normal.

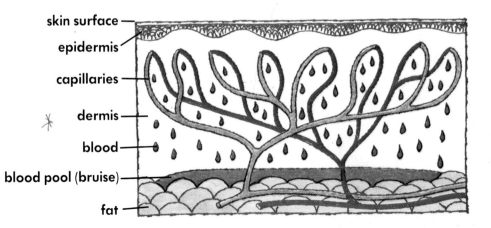

What Makes a Bump?

When you bruise your head or shin, you sometimes get a bump. Why? Because the bone is right beneath the skin in these places, and the skin has to swell outward to make room for the spilled blood.

Sometimes, if you don't bang yourself too hard, you get a bump, but it isn't black and blue. This is because no red cells have leaked out of the blood vessels. Only the clear fluid called plasma has seeped through the vessel walls. A bump forms, but the plasma is quickly absorbed back into the vessels, and the bump soon goes away. Because no red blood cells were spilled, no bruise is left behind.

If you hit a bony place—say your shin—very hard, however, you may bruise the bone itself. Deposits of calcium, a mineral that is part of bone, may form in the bruise, making it hard
to the touch. Such a bruise takes longer to heal and hurts more
than other bruises. Bit by bit, however, white blood cells clear
away the spilled blood and the calcium deposits. Then the
bump goes away and your skin is smooth once again.

What Causes a Nosebleed?

When you get hit in the nose by something hard, you may get a nosebleed. Small blood vessels in the lining of the nose have been damaged. A nosebleed heals just like any other cut: A clot forms, the bleeding stops and the injured area is rebuilt.

Often a person's nose may start bleeding suddenly, and no one knows why. The sensitive lining of the nose may have been damaged by dried mucus from a cold.

Even though it may *look* as if a person is losing a lot of blood from a nosebleed, the actual amount lost is usually small.

How Does a Burn Heal?

While you are baking cookies, you touch the stove and burn yourself. It hurts because skin cells have been destroyed by the heat. The damaged cells release chemicals that stimulate nerves and cause pain.

Burns do not usually bleed, but otherwise they heal the same way cuts do. Often a blister forms, which acts like a scab to cover the hurt area. Under it, white blood cells arrive to attack any bacteria, and a new layer of skin grows in from the edges of the burn.

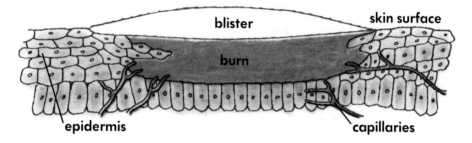

If a burn is very large, or if it goes very deep, it can be dangerous. The skin cells at the edges cannot grow over the burned area fast enough, so bacteria can enter easily and cause infection. In addition, the fluid that forms a large part of the body's cells is left open to the air and can evaporate. When this happens, a burn victim can die.

Doctors treat serious burns like these with skin grafts— patches of healthy skin that are transplanted, or moved, from other areas of the body. To cover very large burns, skin from another person or artificial skin may be used.

How Broken Bones Heal

Bones make a frame to hold us up. They help us walk, sit and stand, and to do this they have to be strong and hard. Bone is hard because two thirds of it is made of hardened non-living minerals—mostly calcium and phosphorus. The other one third of the bone is living material.

When a bone fractures—breaks or cracks—a doctor must line up the pieces and put on a cast so the pieces can't move and the bone will heal straight. But the doctor cannot heal the bone. It is the body itself that does the healing, a process that starts the moment after the break happens.

When a bone is fractured, blood vessels in and around the bone are broken. A large blood clot forms in minutes, surrounding the broken ends of the bone and filling in the space between them.

White blood cells arrive from the bloodstream and begin their usual clean-up campaign. While they are at work, the area is inflamed: red, hot, swollen and painful.

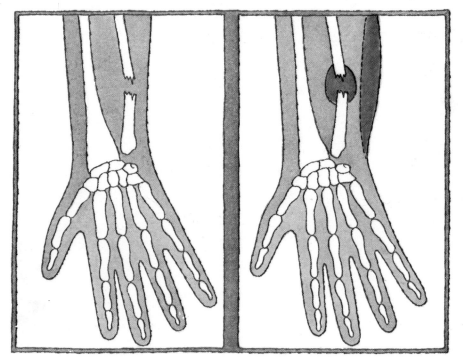

1. *Bone is fractured*   2. *Blood clot forms*

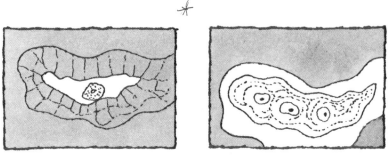

bone-making cell   **bone-destroying cell**

As the white cells are finishing up, two kinds of bone cells become active. One is a bone-making cell. The other is a bone-destroying cell. Both kinds are needed to repair the bone.

The bone-destroying cells are needed because the living part of the bones dies at the jagged edges of the break. Bone-destroying cells dissolve the hard mineral part of the dead bone, leaving the broken ends soft and spongy.

Then the bone-making cells can begin laying down a network of new bone to form a connection between the broken ends. In two or three weeks a bulgy bridge has formed. At this stage the new bone is still soft. If it is moved, it can tear apart. That is why a broken limb is usually put in a cast.

Little by little, the bone-making cells deposit minerals into the network of soft bone. As more and more minerals are de-

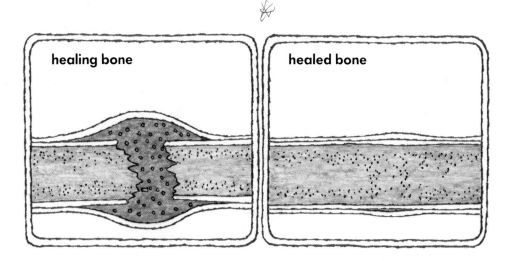

healing bone

healed bone

posited, the bone becomes harder and harder. Eventually, the new bone is as hard as the old.

Then the bone-destroying cells get to work again. They eat away the outside bulges of the bridge. Most broken bones are as good as new in two or three months. In fact, after a bone is fully healed, the broken place often can't be seen, even in an X ray.

What Is a Sprain?

You twist your ankle skating and it hurts so badly you can hardly take a step. Everyone says you must have broken it, and off you go to the emergency room. But X rays show no bones are broken. Instead, the ankle is sprained. This means that a ligament or tendon has been stretched or torn. Ligaments and tendons are tough bands that hold the bones and muscles in place. Sprains happen most often to ligaments or tendons in joints like the knee, ankle and wrist.

Sprains must be kept still so the tear can heal. White cells clean up debris, and fiber-maker cells manufacture scar tissue to mend the torn part. To keep a sprain from moving, a doctor usually bandages it. If the sprain is very bad, it may even need a cast, and the person may have to walk on crutches.

Sprains heal much faster than broken bones do—in about two or three weeks, rather than months.

Reattaching Lost Limbs

When a salamander loses its tail, a new one will grow. But a person who loses a limb can't grow another one. Only a few parts of the human body will regenerate, or grow back, if they're damaged. Among them are the hair and fingernails, the surface layer of the skin, the cells of the liver, and the nerves that run from the spinal cord to other parts of the body. (If the nerve cells inside the brain and spinal cord are destroyed, however, they cannot regenerate.)

In past times, when a limb was cut off in an accident, nothing could be done to save it. Even if a doctor did try to sew the limb on again, the blood vessels and nerves could not be reconnected. Scar tissue would soon form between the cut ends of the vessels and nerves. Without connected nerves, the limb could not move or feel. Without a flow of blood, the limb would die.

Today, however, doctors can often reattach a limb successfully by doing microsurgery—performing an operation under a special microscope. Using tiny surgical instruments that look as if they belong in a dollhouse, doctors sew together the blood vessels and the nerves.

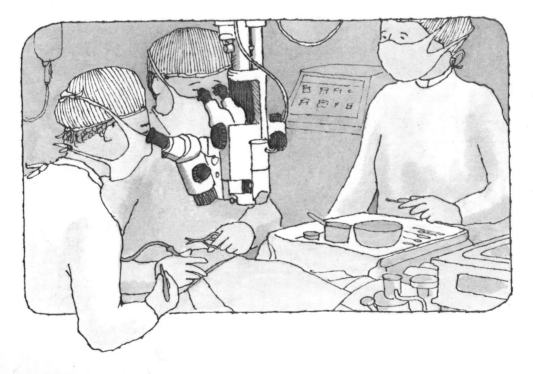

Blood begins flowing to the reattached limb at once. But it takes a few weeks or months for the nerves to grow back. When they do, they do not always work perfectly. This is because there are hundreds of tiny nerve fibers inside every nerve. When a nerve is sewn together, some of these fibers may get crossed. Eventually, however, the nerves usually regenerate well enough so the person can use the limb again.

*   *   *

Everyone gets little cuts and scrapes. They heal quickly, and we usually don't think much about it. But even though we take the healing process for granted, our life would not be possible without it. Even small injuries would be life threatening: They would stay open to infection and damage would never be repaired.

We think of doctors as healers, and doctors can help the body heal. But in the end, it is the body itself that makes its own repairs through the amazing healing process.

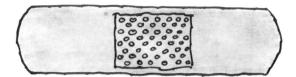

First Aid for Minor Injuries

Remember, with any injury the first thing to do is to tell an adult at once. Here are some simple first-aid steps every family should know.

CUTS AND SCRAPES
- Press cut with clean cloth or fingers until bleeding stops.
- Wash cut with soap and water.
- Pat dry with a clean towel.
- Leave cut open to air. (Creams, ointments and Band-Aids are usually not needed. If you must use a Band-Aid, change it often.)

Get Medical Help If:
- the edges of the cut don't come together;
- you can't stop the bleeding;
- you can't wash out all the dirt in the cut;
- the cut is made by an animal bite;
- the cut is a small deep hole made by a sharp object like a nail;
- the cut becomes infected: very red, swollen, painful, hot and full of pus;
- you see red lines or streaks leading from the cut;
- you get a fever along with an infected cut;
- the cut doesn't look better in two or three days.

NOSEBLEEDS
- Sit down and lean forward (leaning back may cause you to choke).

- Pinch your nostrils closed and breathe through your mouth. (Keep pinching on and off for about 5 minutes, or until bleeding stops.)
- Do not blow your nose for about 12 hours.

See a doctor if bleeding does not stop after 15 minutes.

BRUISES AND BUMPS
For a swollen, painful bruise:
- Apply an icebag or a cold, moist cloth for about 10 minutes to lessen pain and swelling.
- After the first day, use a warm, moist cloth to speed healing.

BURNS
- AT ONCE: hold burn under cold water (not ice water).
- Keep in cold water for 10 minutes.
- Do not put any grease, butter or cream on a burn.
- If a blister does form, do not break it.
- If a blister breaks, wash area with soap and water and cover with a Band-Aid.

For a severe burn, get medical help.

BROKEN BONES OR SPRAINS
- Keep a broken or sprained limb still.
- Don't walk on the limb.
- Tell an adult at once.
- Get medical help quickly.

Important:
- DO NOT try to force broken bones into a different position!
- DO NOT move someone who has an injured back or neck!

Index

Numbers in *italics* refer to drawings.

0